Bee Lessons

Think bees,
Thank natural life,
And bee happy.

Howard Scott

Howard Scott's Other Books:
    Change From Within
    Fighting Money

ISBN Number 1-57087-524-3
Library of Congress Control Number 2002103174

Professional Press
Chapel Hill, NC 27515-4371

Manufactured in the United States of America
        04 05 06   10 9 8 7 6 5 4 3

Instead of dirt and poison, we have chosen to fill our hives with honey and wax; thus furnishing mankind with the two noblest of things, which are sweetness and light.

— Jonathan Swift

Introduction

In my years as a beekeeper, I have come to the conclusion that we can learn much from these insects. It's not that honeybees are so wise, although they have been around for 6 million years, and it's not sure we will achieve that longevity. Rather, I come to my conclusions from reflecting on both our worlds and seeing the way bees exist in harmony with nature. In this little book, I present some of those lessons.

Bee Life

Bees live naturally in the wild or are artificially kept by beekeepers. Simply put, we put a box over them and let them do their thing. Either way, they devote their lives to the hive. That's the miracle of bees—complete subjugation of the individual for the group.

Lesson 1:
It's satisfying to work for the greater good.

Bee Love

In a hive, there is one queen. A few thousand male drones, and 40,000 to 50,000 undeveloped female workers. The female workers all get along. They work together, hang out together, eat together, and defend against enemies. The cooperation stems from their love of the hive and their willingness to be part of a large family. The fact that it is a female-oriented society probably helps.

Lesson 2:

Leave it to females to run things well.

Home Sweet Hexagon

A bee's home is a hexagon-shaped wax cell. Sheets of cells form comb, where thousands of bees live. Bees build these sheet structures from wax they secrete from abdominal glands. In the wild, they fill all available space, allowing just enough room to move around the combs. The sheets hang on branches, occupy cavities in trees, and of course, form on frames supplied by beekeepers. The hexagon cells are all-purpose compartments for food storage, brood-rearing, eating, and resting.

Lesson 3:
The perfect living space is a hexagon.

Bee Space

Man's beehive takes into account the 3/8" bee space. Every frame is aligned so that there is exactly 3/8" separating side, top and bottom. Any less space, and the bees can't easily move around. Any more space, and the bees build comb, which could block man's access. In the natural world, bees build their rows of comb 3/8" apart.

Lesson 4:
Good spaces make good neighbors.

The System

Bees are great engineers. They create a working system of circulation, moisture control, and air flow. If possible, they bore air vents in the top and bottom of the hive. They fan their wings to move the air around. They also keep their home dry by fanning. They create heat by shivering. Otherwise, the hive would become damp, close, hot, or cold, causing disease.

Lesson 5:
You don't have to go to college to understand thermodynamics.

The Sun Imperative

Bees eat, live, work, and die by the sun. On bright mornings, they emerge from their hive at a fever pitch and fly as far as three miles away to gather nectar and pollen. Then, using the sun as a sort of radar, they find their way back. Bees rely on the sun to keep their hive warm, to keep down moisture, and to keep honey liquid. In winter, the sun also provides warmth.

Lesson 6:
Embrace the sun. It's the life force.

Work Ethic

The hive devotes itself to filling up every available cell with honey. After the queen lays eggs in the center of each frame, the bees fill surrounding cells with nectar and evaporate it into honey. When the bees fill up two brood tiers with 50 pounds of honey, beekeepers put on a queen excluder and add a third tier. Because the queen can't fit through the barrier, she can't lay eggs there. So the bees fill the tier with honey. As one tier is being filled, another is added. In a good year, a beekeeper harvests 150 pounds.

Lesson 7:
Given a challenge, rise to the occasion.

The Division of Labor

The diversity of jobs within a beehive is quite remarkable. There are housekeepers, brood rearers, guards, food processors, builders, queen tenders, foragers, scouts, storers, transporters, and cappers. Looking into a hive, one thinks chaos. But every insect is focused on a task. There is an organization as controlled as any factory.

Lesson 8:
By dividing up the work, more gets done.

Variety is Best

Tasks are age-related, so that every worker bee does many jobs during a lifetime. She starts cleaning cells, then processes honey, then tends the queen, then guards the entrance, and finally forages for nectar and pollen. By some mysterious process, she learns what to do. Evidently, age is the key to experience. Moreover, she does each job with enthusiasm, working 24-hour days, taking short naps. There's never any problem with slackers.

Lesson 9:
The best way to achieve job satisfaction is variety.

Of Passion and Sex

The queen takes off on her one mating voyage out of the hive. It's called the nuptial flight. She flies skyward. There, thousands of drones wait. The queen mates with 15 or 20 drones, whose internal organs immediately rupture. They suffer instant death. The remaining drones, who aren't as aggressive, return to the hive and enjoy an abundant spring and summer, living off the honey surplus and the labor of others.

Lesson 10:
In love, it is best to be cautious.

Just Reward

The drones do no work, but gorge them-selves on honey. Getting fat and ungainly, they continually bump into workers. By summer's end, the workers, realizing that they've been supporting these idle slobs, throw the drones out of the hive. Pulling them out by force, they often tear off a leg or rip a wing, spelling doom for these party boys.

Lesson 11:
Mooching doesn't pay.

Regal Leadership

The queen is the most remarkable figure in the hive. She is the spirit and lifeforce. She lays upwards of 2,000 eggs a day. She leads by pheromones—that is by issuing chemical substances which the bees sense. If she's in danger, every worker bee will give up its life to save her. When she abandons the hive, many workers follow. If she dies suddenly, the hive must quickly create a new queen or perish.

Lesson 12:
Long live the Queen.

Queen Ministration

The queen is always surrounded by attendants. They circle her, keeping her clean, providing her with food, fanning her with cool air, keeping her dry, discarding her eliminations, and combing her. Through combing, they also convey her wishes by spreading her pheromone emanations. About the only thing the queen never has is privacy.

Lesson 13:
Being the leader has its downside.

Balling the Queen

When the bees decide to dispose of a queen, for whatever reason, they ball her to death. That means encircling and smothering her and tearing at her body parts until she can not move. For example, if a new queen is introduced too quickly into the hive, she will usually be balled.

Lesson 14:
History is made in an impetuous moment.

The Honey Factory

Consider the beehive as an enormous factory. Forager bees bring in nectar and pollen. In their stomachs, they've already started breaking down the sugars of the nectar. At the entrance, transport bees take the nectar through their proboscises and deposit it in cells. Foragers then stuff pollen balls in inner cells near brood, because pollen is food for the young. Processor bees fan the liquid nectar, reducing water content to 17%. Finally, capper bees cap the thickened nectar when it becomes honey.

Lesson 15:
Only a magical food could be made from such an intricate, involved process.

'Busy as a Bee'

Bees are super industrious. When the sun is shining, they work from sunup to sundown seven days a week. When flying great distances, they never stop to rest. Even when resting, they often do something, like fan their wings to keep the air moving. In fact, in summer, most bees die prematurely in six or seven weeks, because they wear out their wings, not lose their energy.

Lesson 16:
Hard work costs, but the ride's the thing.

A Pointed Tale

A bee will only sting when the hive or her life is threatened. Upon stinging, the bee tries to pull out its barbed stinger. Instead, it tugs out its entrails and dies. So giving its life to save the colony is a true Kamikaze gesture. How bees are bred for such self-sacrifice is a mystery, but perhaps that's why they've been around for 6 million years.

Lesson 17:
Loyalty is the key to group survival.

The Purest Pain

When a bee stings, it hurts alot. It's painful going in, because the stinger is sharp and stiff. It hurts going out, because the bee struggles unsuccessfully to pull out her barbed stinger. Instead, she rips open her body. It throbs for three days because the injected poison swells muscles and inhibits movement.

Lesson 18:
The smallest stinger packs a potent punch.

Cold Weather Solution

In the winter, bees form a bowling-ball cluster. Like PacMan, the sphere moves around the hive, eating honey stores. The center of the cluster, where the queen resides, is kept at a constant 92 degrees, when she starts to lay eggs in February. Bees expand or contract the sphere to maintain a steady, radiating warmth.

Lesson 19:
When it's cold outside, huddle with loved ones.

Shivering

Bees provide heat by shivering. By moving body muscles, energy radiates out. And by huddling close together, this energy is turned into heat. Even bees at the outer surface of the cluster have enough warmth to survive.

Lesson 20:
Shiver and stay warm.

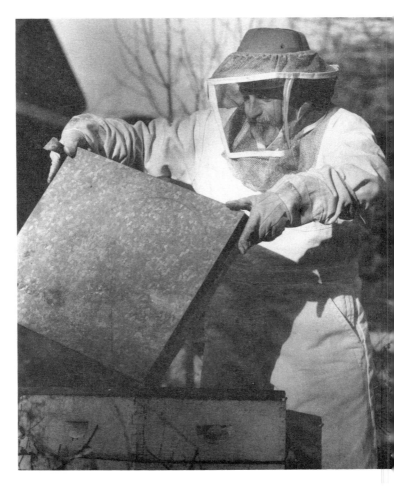

Winter Cleansing

On a sunny, mid-winter day, when the temperature rises above 50 degrees, the bees uncluster and come out for a winter cleansing. Often they haven't gone to the bathroom for weeks, and they leave their yellow imprint in the snow. Their pleasure at being outside, if only for a short while, is evident.

Lesson 21:
If you have to go...

Why Revolutions Happen

Development of the hive is a delicate balance between food accumulation, brood creation, and disease prevention. When the queen begins to produce fewer eggs, the balance breaks down. Sensing flagging leadership, the workers create a new queen by feeding extra dosages of royal jelly to several cells. Instead of a worker, a new queen emerges. The workers kill her mother, the old queen, and destroy the other cells. The new queen assumes absolute leadership, and begins to lay 2,000 eggs a day herself.

Lesson 22:
A loss of confidence is what triggers a revolution.

The Replacement Principle

When the workers decide to replace an aging queen, they spread extra amounts of royal jelly over normal egg cells. Small quantities of this royal jelly is used to feed normal cells. Extra amounts turn a worker egg into a queen egg. To be safe, the bees apply the substance to a dozen cells at staggared duration dates. That way, if one queen doesn't make it, another will. When a new queen emerges, the first act of the hive is to destroy all the other queen cells.

Lesson 23:
Produce more heirs than you need to insure survival.

The Swarming Impulse

When a hive gets crowded or is losing the battle with disease, the bees think about swarming. They first create new queen cells. When the workers are tending these royal cells, before a new leader hatches, the old queen leaves with half to two-thirds the hive. This is a swarm. The swarm often clusters on a nearby tree, while scouts seek a permanent home. When scouts find one, the swarm takes off in the form of a huge cloud to its new residence.

Lesson 24:
Sometimes one has to leave home to make things work.

The Spirit of Defense

When outside bees try to rob a hive, guard bees attack them and fight them away. If necessary, the guards will get reinforcements, by issuing scent alarms. If a mouse enters the hive, the bees will mass together and try to sting it or build a propolis wall around its nest. Bees will always risk their lives to save the hive.

Lesson 25:
Dulcet et decorum est pro patria Mori.
(Sweet and beautiful it is to die for one's country).

Storing the Bounty

Among all the animal and insect world, only honeybees systematically store food to last the winter. In fact, the storing imperative is their strongest instinct. A hive will often store three to four times what it needs. Why these little insects are one of the few creatures that believe in saving for a rainy day is truly a mystery.

Lesson 26:
Surplus insures survival.

Flower Work

All bees get to work outdoors. Foraging for nectar and pollen is the last job they do. How pleasant to work outside when the sun is shining. All day, they get to smell flowers and suck up nectar. They mingle with friends, amid the buzz and hum of fellow insects. Listening to their exuberant humming, you can tell they're enjoying themselves.

Lesson 27:
There's no better place to work than around flowers.

The Pollination Miracle

Forager bees go from flower to flower sucking out nectar and gathering balls of pollen on their legs. Covered with the yellow sticky substance, they leave bits at each stop. In the process, they transfer pollen to the stigma, the female organ of flowers. This serendipitous act increases flora and gives us more bountiful crops. About one-third of all crops are pollinated by honeybees.

Lesson 28:
Nature loves serendipity.

The Power of Smell

The bees' most important sense is smell. They catch robbers by smell, detecting a different odor on their bodies. They use smell to find flowers. They find the queen by smell. When smoked by a beekeeper, they respond by fleeing deep into the hive. When they sting, they give off an odor warning others of danger.

Lesson 29:
It's all in the schnoz (antennae).

The Bee Dance

On the combs inside the hive, a forager bee does a dance. It's a wiggling, gyrating motion called a waggle dance. This movement is more than entertainment. It communicates the whereabouts of nectar finds. Through her gyrations, the bee spells out, in Morse code-fashion, how to get from here to there in the air.

Lesson 30:
Nothing conveys a message like dance.

Hanging Out

On hot nights, bees hang out. They drape over the hive entrance and crawl up the front. They rest from their work. They listen to night sounds. They flex their bodies. They buzz in contentment. They catch the balmy breeze of a hot summer's night.

Lesson 31:
After a hard day's work, it's good to relax.

Bee Vision

A bee has three simple and two compound eyes. She sees fuzzy images of the same thing from different angles. She also can detect air flow. She uses her sight to orient herself and to avoid bumping into objects, while moving at fast speed. Such a mistake could be costly, as the impact might provoke a sting and cause death.

Lesson 32:
Sharp eyes are critical for fast-moving creatures.

Nature's Beauty

There is true beauty in the world of bees. There's the symmetrical beauty of a hexagon cell. There's the delicate beauty of a perfectly-capped frame full of honey. There is the architectural beauty of the intricate hive structure, with its narrow pathways and propolized fissures. There's the swirling beauty of the golden liquid. Finally, there's the primal beauty of a swarm.

Lesson 33:
Beauty appears in many different forms.

The Virtue of Simplicity

Like Thoreau, bees believe in simplicity. Only the essences matter. They eat one food and are nourished. They live in a simple cell. The take pleasure in doing routine tasks over and over. They never want more than what's in front of them. Finally, they never wonder what it all means.

Lesson 34:
In simplicity, there is peace.

The Joy of Honey

Honey is an amazing food. The ingredients are nectar from flowers and enzymes added by the bees. Bees then fan the nectar, evaporating it into honey. Unlike most foodstuffs, honey doesn't need refrigeration. It will never gather mold. It lasts forever. In fact, honey was used in ancient Egypt to embalm kings. If it crystallizes, heating restores its texture. That's why it's called nectar of the gods and why it's considered nature's pure food.

Lesson 35:
Mother Nature provides the healthiest nourishment.

Honey Drops

Because it is made drop by drop, honey is a remarkable food. One bee contributes 1/8 teaspoon in her lifetime. Bees travel the equivalent of two and one-half times around the world to create one pound of honey. Moreover, because it's local, honey always has a distinctive color, aroma, and flavor.

Lesson 36:
Something so delicious must be made delicately.

Honey Variety

Honey color varies from almost translucent amber to molasses black. Odors range from a slight smell to a cloying density of nature. Some people say that they can taste individual flowers in honey and identify them. Viscosity also changes with the season and with the type of honey.

Lesson 37:
True variety is in subtle distinctions.

Bee By-products

Besides honey, bees collect and use several other substances. They gather pollen from flowers and feed to young bees as food. They secrete wax from abdomen glands, which is used to build comb. They gather propolis from tree sap and use as glue and filler. Man, in turn, uses honey as a sweetener, pollen as a health supplement, and wax to make candles and ornaments.

Lesson 38:
Waste nothing.

A Beehive's History

Abeehive can go on for years and years. One queen passes the mantle to another, and two years later, that queen might be replaced. Each queen presides over dozens of generations of bees, who live six weeks in summer or several months in the winter. After a while, comb turns brown. Living hives up to 40 years old have been found.

Lesson 39:
History is written on the walls.

Death of the Beehive

A dead hive is a terrible sight to behold. You open the hive and see a cluster of inert insects huddled together. Others cling to the cells. Often, there's a charnel odor or foul smell in the case of disease. The silence is unnerving. You think: where once there was teeming life is now nothing. And always, you wonder—what happened?

Lesson 40:
Death, even insect death, makes you pause.

Sign of Spring

Besides robins and croci, bees are an important sign of spring. Sightings of active bees proclaim that the insects have made it through another harsh winter and that the greening of the country-side will soon begin.

Lesson 41:
Ah, bees. Ah, life.

Bee Stories

I love to hear bee stories. One person told me about how, as a boy, his father taught him to reach into an old tree hole at night and grab honey chunks without getting stung. Another individual spoke of attending a beekeeper friend's funeral. After spying several honeybees above the grave, he realized that his pal was okay. A beekeeper told me an incident of swallowing a bee in his coffee, being stung in the esophagus, and, laughing about it after recovering.

Lesson 42:
Keep the magic going. Tell bee stories.

Howard Scott, beekeeper, began keeping bees 20 years ago. He is a frequent contributor to *American Bee Journal* and *Bee Culture*. His real interest is the poetical wonder of bees.